WHITEWATERCOOKS

pure, simple and real creations from the Fresh Tracks Cafe

whitecap

Whitecap Books Ltd., Suite 210–314 West Cordova Street, Vancouver
British Columbia, Canada V6B 1E8 | www.whitecap.ca

Photography: David R. Gluns
Introduction Photograph: Peter Moynes
Chef: Shelley Adams
Food Stylist: Shelley Adams
Editors: Shelley Adams and Joanne Ryan
Introduction by: Sean McGinnis
Original Concept by: Shelley Adams and Lori McGinnis
Layout and Design by Prefix Media Inc., Nelson BC
www.prefixmedia.com

Printed and bound in China

Library and Archives Canada Cataloguing in Publication
Adams, Shelley, 1958—
        Whitewater cooks: pure, simple and real creations from the
Fresh Tracks Cafe / Shelley Adams ; David R. Gluns, photographer.

ISBN 1-55285-871-5
ISBN 978-1-55285-871-4
        1. Cookery.   I. Title

TX714.A445 2006   64.15   C2006-904100-8

The publisher acknowledges the financial support of the Government of Canada
through the Canada Book Fund (CBF) and the province of British Columbia
through the Book Publishing Tax Credit.

To order a copy of this book, visit our website at
 www.skiwhitewater.com / www.whitecap.ca or call 1-800-666-9420

For my unique and very creative mother, Bernice...

...whose love of beautiful and delicious food has been passed on to me - the only kid in school eating crab stuffed avocados for lunch!!

CONTENTS

creations from the Fresh Tracks Cafe!

ACKNOWLEDGEMENTS

thanks to all of you

This book has been a marvellous journey that began a few years ago in a local school playground. My friend suggested I take all those delicious recipes from the Fresh Tracks Café, some of the fabulous recipes from my catering days, cooking school days and dinner party days and put them all together in a cookbook. She offered to type and to help and to do whatever it takes to make it happen. Just as long as she could have a copy for her kitchen. Without her tireless efforts, encouragement and sense of humour, the first step of this book would never have been taken. Thanks to Lori!

Of course I'd like to thank so many amazing cooks I have worked with. Thanks to , M.E. McKnight, Gail Morrison, Marianne Abraham, Linda Klein, Anni Bailey, Val Grlic, Cathy Crooks, Pat McInnis, to all the great Whitewater kitchen staff who have contributed to the success of our Fresh Tracks Cafe...and especially to the very dedicated and talented Joanne Ryan who made this book possible in the end! Thank you!!

Thanks so much to the incredible girls who designed this book, Minn and Tara of Prefix Media Inc. You are both so talented and patient!

Finally, to my adorable family who have listened to me for several years talk about "The Book". Your opinions, understanding, and recipe testing have been very cherished. Thanks Mike, Ali and Conner...I love you guys.

INTRODUCTION

In kayak, canoe and rafting circles, the term "Whitewater" elicits images of raging rivers surging over boulders, crashing over falls and thundering down tree-lined chutes. Shake off your jacket, brush the snow off your goggles and you'll find yourself at Whitewater Winter Resort, snuggled within the craggy peaks of the Selkirk Mountain Range, some 21 km south of Nelson, British Columbia. Nelson is known throughout the skiing world for its artistic flair, heritage buildings and its passion for caffeine and powder snow. Come to Nelson for the coffee; stay for the powder… oh, and bring a snow blower.

With a base elevation of 5400 feet and a summit elevation of 6700 feet, Whitewater receives an average annual snowfall of 40-50 feet of dry Kootenay powder. Ymir peak, at an elevation of 8000 feet provides a spectacular focal point to Whitewater basin, soaring above the clouds to imbue skiers with its majestic spirit. Aside from over 700 acres of incredible tree, glade   and unparalleled powder skiing, Whitewater also offers its guests delicious meals that have long been the envy of ski resorts across North America.

After a mind-blowing powder run through Catch Basin, Terra Ratta, or Sproulers, many a snow-encrusted skier has stumbled into the lodge and ploughed into a piece of heaven like a Ymir Curry Bowl or a Whiskey Smoked Salmon Chowder from Whitewater's extensive gourmet menu at the Fresh Tracks Café. "For the love of God," they moan in ecstasy, "You must give me the recipe."

Alas, until now the gourmet recipes made famous at Whitewater were as unattainable as a snowflake in July. So guarded were some of the ingredients that employees had to swear an oath of secrecy before being allowed in or out of the kitchen. Legend has it that more than one former kitchen worker who could not keep the faith lies beneath the floorboards of "Coal Oil Johnny's".

After much consternation, the veil has been lifted and the general public now has the opportunity to rustle up a touch of Whitewater heaven in the privacy of their own kitchens. With the help of this guide-book, you can now enjoy the magic of the Whitewater menu twelve months a year. To those of you who have begged for years for the ingredients to the Whitewater Burger Sauce, we say, "stop phoning". To those of you who love a little magic in your Monday, who sleep with your skis from September to April, who appreciate the difference between coriander and cilantro, we say, "Whitewater cooks, Bon Appetit".

WHITEWATER HISTORY

Whitewater Ski Area was discovered when two local Nelson businessmen, exploring backcountry mountain roads on motorcycles, pulled over for a break and spotted what appeared to be a natural ski bowl tucked into the hidden peaks of the Selkirk Range.

In 1969 the two men, together with the Silver King Ski Club, initiated the development of the Whitewater basin, at the foot of Ymir peak. The project was supported and financed by the club, the province, and the good people of Nelson, who volunteered almost 9,000 hours of work over five years (close to what the current owners, Mike and Shelley Adams, log each ski season).

Over the next six years, the ski facilities were installed. The famous Whitewater lodge was designed by a local architect and completed in October, 1974. The following year, two Riblet chairs (Riblet Lifts Co. originated in Nelson) were installed.

In 1986, a small herd of local skiing enthusiasts pooled their meagre resources to purchase the ski area from the Ski Society. Their goals were to offer a safe and enjoyable ski experience at an affordable price while continuing to improve and expand the ski area.

In 1992 Whitewater purchased the infamous "Olive Chair" from Whistler. The following year the T-bar was removed, and Whitewater's new Silver King Chair was installed. A downtown Nelson office was opened in September of 1993 to better serve Whitewater's growing powder-hound population.

During the summer of 1997 the last of the Riblet lifts, the Hummingbird Chair, was removed and the Hummer Handle Tow was installed to provide lift serviced beginner terrain (the "bunny hill").

The same year, Shelley and Mike Adams won the right to purchase the ski area from the previous owners in a now legendary game of high stakes Scrabble. Shelley and Mike continue to offer a philosophy of providing a safe and enjoyable ski experience at an affordable price, with "all you can eat" powder.

An additional 80 acres of skiable glades were added to Whitewater in 2003 when a major boundary expansion took place. With the launch of a twenty-year master expansion plan in 2003, the future of the ski area was ensured.

Whitewater has been recognized in national and international magazines for the quaintness of its setting, the quantity of its powder and the quality of its food.

Taste the mountain. Come to your senses at Whitewater.

SOUPS and BOWLS
a selection of our best sellers

MINESTRONE SOUP

This may be the ultimate hearty vegetable soup.

serves 8

INGREDIENTS

4 slices bacon or prosciutto, sliced into small pieces

2 tbsp butter

4 cloves garlic, finely minced

2 carrots diced

1 large onion diced

1 leek (white part and a bit of the green) cut in half lengthwise then sliced thinly

3 cups shredded green cabbage

2 zucchini quartered lengthwise, then cut into 1/4 inch pieces

1 potato, peeled and diced

4 cups chicken stock

2 cups beef stock

2 tbsp tomato paste

1 cup dry red wine

5 tbsp chopped Italian parsley

2 tsp dried oregano

3 tbsp fresh chopped basil

1 tsp black pepper

salt, to taste

1-14 oz tin red kidney beans drained and rinsed

4 fresh tomatoes, diced

1/2 cup small pasta (macaroni or small bow shape)

1/2 cup fresh parmesan cheese, for garnish

METHOD

Fry bacon pieces in large soup pot until cooked. Add the butter, garlic, carrots, onion, and leek. Sauté until vegetables are translucent. Add cabbage, zucchini, potato, stocks, wine and tomato paste. Bring to a boil. Reduce heat and add oregano, 2 tbsp parsley, salt and pepper. Simmer another 15-20 minutes. Add the kidney beans, tomatoes, and pasta. Cook until pasta is done. Adjust seasonings, and add the rest of the parsley and the basil. Serve with the parmesan cheese.

ROASTED THREE TOMATO PESTO SOUP

A beautiful Tuscan inspired soup.

serves 12-16

INGREDIENTS

12 fresh tomatoes, quartered and roasted
1/4 cup balsamic vinegar
2 tbsp brown sugar
1/2 cup olive oil
4 cloves garlic
3 large onions, diced
1 1/2 cups sun-dried tomatoes, chopped

2-28 oz cans crushed tomatoes
6 cups vegetable stock
1 cup red wine
1/4 cup dried basil
1 bunch fresh basil, julienned
1/2 cup pesto, store bought is fine
parmesan or asiago cheese to garnish

METHOD

Toss tomatoes and garlic cloves with balsamic vinegar, brown sugar and half of the olive oil and roast in a 350°F oven for 30 minutes. In a large soup pot, heat remaining oil and sauté onions until softened and slightly caramelized. Add crushed tomatoes, stock, sun-dried tomatoes and red wine. Let simmer for 20 minutes. Add roasted tomatoes and garlic cloves, dried basil and boil for five minutes. Purée in food processor and add fresh basil and pesto. Ladle into bowls and sprinkle with parmesan or asiago cheese.

Slices of "Au Soleil Levant" baguette, brushed with olive oil and crumbled goat cheese, quickly toasted in the oven, make a beautiful garnish.

WHISKEYSMOKED**SALMON**CHOWDER

A personal favourite of Steve Flett...could it be the whiskey?

serves 10-12

INGREDIENTS

1/4 cup butter

2 onions, chopped finely

6 celery stocks, chopped finely

8 red or white potatoes, peeled and diced

1/2 cup chopped fresh fennel bulb or 1/2 teaspoon fennel seeds

2 cups milk

2 cups fish stock or clam nectar

2 1/2 cups corn

1 cup whipping cream

1 small tin tomato paste

1 teaspoon lobster base (optional)

1 pound smoked salmon, cut into small pieces (barbequed salmon tips work well too)

juice and zest of one lemon

1 bunch fresh dill, chopped

2 ounces Jack Daniel's Bourbon

a pinch of saffron threads (optional)

salt and pepper to taste

METHOD

In heavy bottomed soup pot, sauté onions, celery and saffron (if using) in butter. Add potatoes and fennel. Sauté briefly, then pour in milk and stock. Add a little salt and pepper and cover. Let simmer on medium heat until potatoes are soft, approximately 20 minutes. Add corn, cream, tomato paste and lobster base. Cook 5 minutes more and then finish soup with smoked salmon, lemon juice, lemon zest, fresh dill and...whiskey!

Lobster Base, a delicious pot of flavour to have in your freezer. Made by Minors and available at any food wholesaler. Keep frozen and dig a spoon in as needed. Also excellent in pasta sauces. Saffron threads can be found at the Kootenay Co-op. Use only a pinch, as flavour is very intense.

THAICOCONUTANDCHICKENSOUP

A local artist and avid skier, Maria Medina, shared this recipe with me years ago. It's turned into a favourite with our dedicated regulars.

serves 8

INGREDIENTS

4 cups coconut milk
2 cups chicken stock
6 fresh or dried kaffir lime leaves
3 pieces dried galangal root
1 tbsp lemon juice
1 tbsp fish sauce
1 tbsp sugar

1 tbsp lemongrass, diced in 1 inch pieces
2 tsp roasted chili paste
1 cup cooked chicken breast, cut into bite sized pieces
2 cups fresh mushrooms, sliced
2 carrots, julienned
1 red pepper, julienned
fresh cilantro, chopped

METHOD

In a large soup pot, bring coconut milk and stock to a boil. Add kaffir lime leaves, galangal root, lemon juice, fish sauce, sugar, chili paste and lemongrass. Simmer for 5 minutes. Add chicken, mushrooms, carrots, red pepper, and simmer another 10 minutes. Taste and add more lemon juice, sugar or fish sauce as needed. Garnish with chopped cilantro.

Served on a bowl of cooked and cooled rice noodles makes a heartier soup! Kaffir lime leaves and roasted chili paste can both be found at Ellison's Market in Nelson.

BABA'S BORSCHT

My dear friend Joanne Ryan has a real Baba for a mother-in-law. This is her recipe for the classic Russian soup that is familiar and comforting to so many Kootenay folks. Thank you Baba!

makes 10 qts of soup

INGREDIENTS

3 cans diced tomatoes (28 oz size)
2 medium beets, cut into 6 pieces
10 potatoes, 6 cut in half and 4 cubed
6 quarts of water

1/2 cup butter
1 small bunch celery, diced
2 medium onions, diced
1 small green pepper, diced
3 cloves garlic, grated finely
1 medium sized head, shredded cabbage
4 cups carrots, diced

1 small head cauliflower, diced
1 1/2 cups diced yellow or green beans (optional)
1 1/2 cups of whipping cream
1/2 cup fresh dill, finely chopped
salt and pepper to taste

METHOD

Put water, beets, halved potatoes, and half of the tomatoes in a large pot and bring to the boil. Melt butter in large pot and add celery, onions, green pepper and garlic. Cook over medium heat until softened, but not browned. Add remaining tomatoes and half of the cabbage. Cook stirring often until cabbage is done and the tomatoes are reduced and thick. When potatoes in the pot are cooked, remove them and the beets. Discard the beets; Mash the potatoes with the cream. Add the mashed potatoes to the cooked celery, onion, cabbage mixture and stir over low heat. When you remove the large potatoes, add the carrots, diced potatoes and rest of the cabbage. Cook for about 10 minutes, and then add the cauliflower and beans. When all the vegetables are tender, mix the two pots together, add more cream to taste and bring to a boil. Add salt, pepper and dill. Makes about 10 quarts.

...Good luck! The method in this recipe seems a little eccentric, but it's authentic and the way Baba makes it!

CARIBBEAN SQUASH SOUP

A real hit, especially during Beach Party Weekend.

serves 8

INGREDIENTS

1 tbsp oil

1 onion, diced

3 cloves garlic, minced

1 fresh jalapeno, seeded and chopped finely

5 cups vegetable stock or water

2 cups butternut squash, peeled and cubed

2 tbsp dark rum

1/4 tsp allspice

4 cups spinach leaves, julienned

1 cup coconut milk

salt and pepper to taste

METHOD

In a large soup pot, sauté onion, garlic, and jalapeno in oil. Add stock, squash, rum, and allspice. Simmer until squash is tender. Puree until smooth. Add spinach leaves and coconut milk. Simmer another 5 minutes, season to taste with salt and pepper. Add a splash more dark rum at the end!

Garnish with julienned spinach leaves and toasted coconut!

BOUILLABAISSE

This recipe originated from a book my mother gave me when I graduated from high school. My fate was sealed! We serve this as a special treat during the Christmas Holidays.

serves 12-14

INGREDIENTS

approximately 3 lbs of fish, cubed (salmon, halibut, red snapper, cod...)

2 dozen mussels or clams, rinsed

2 lbs prawns or lobster meat if you have it

2 quarts good quality fish stock or clam nectar

2 cups dry white wine

4 tbsp butter

4 tbsp olive oil

3 leeks, chopped

1 fennel bulb, chopped

3 celery stocks, chopped

4 cloves garlic, finely diced

2 onions, chopped

1/4 cup parsley, chopped

4 tbsp tomato paste

1 lb fresh tomatoes, diced into small pieces

2 bay leaves

1 tsp thyme

1 tsp fennel seed

2 pinches saffron threads

zest and juice of 1/2 orange

salt and pepper to taste

splash of Pernod or other liquorice flavoured liquor

METHOD

In a large soup pot, sauté leeks, celery, fennel, garlic, and onions in butter and oil until soft. Add bay leaves, thyme, fennel seed, and tomato paste. Sauté another 5 minutes. Add fish stock, tomatoes, and wine. Bring to a medium boil. Add fish pieces, saffron, and orange zest and juice, cook for a few minutes, then mussels, clams, and prawns. When clams open, the soup is done. Turn off and add Pernod, salt and pepper to taste.

Enjoy this with baguettes from our local French Bakery..."Au Soleil Levant".

HUNGARIAN MUSHROOM **BARLEY** SOUP

We sell bowl after bowl of this hearty soup.

serves about 12

INGREDIENTS

2-3 onions, diced

3 tbsp butter

1 tbsp olive oil

1/2 cup barley

1/2 cup sherry

1 tsp pepper

2 tsp fresh rosemary

2 tsp dill

2 tsp paprika

2 tsp salt

12 cups mushrooms, sliced

8 cups vegetable stock

4 bay leaves

1/2 cup parsley

1 tbsp soy sauce

1 cup whipping cream

METHOD

Heat oil and butter in a large soup pot. Add the onions and sauté until translucent. Add mushrooms and sauté another 10-15 minutes. Add the barley and spices and continue to sauté for 10 more minutes. Add the stock and let cook over medium heat approximately 30 minutes or until the barley is done. Add soy sauce, sherry, cream, and parsley.

An added splash of sherry at the end is a must. For a thicker soup, add 2 tbsp flour mixed with 2 tbsp butter and cook a little longer until it thickens up.

YMIRCURRYBOWL

Named after our prettiest peak at Whitewater, skied by all those brave enough and eaten by hundreds of happy customers!

serves 8-10

INGREDIENTS

2 tbsp vegetable oil

2 onions, diced

3 carrots, diced

1 tbsp garlic, minced

1 tbsp ginger, minced

1 red pepper, diced

1 tbsp red curry paste

2 tsp garam masala

2 tsp ground cumin

3 medium potatoes, diced

2 yams, diced

1 tbsp sliced galangal root

1 stalk lemongrass, chopped finely or
 left in large removable piece

3 kaffir lime leaves

2 tbsp fish sauce

juice and zest of 2 limes

3-14 oz cans coconut milk

1-19 oz can chickpeas, drained and rinsed

stock or water, approximately 2 cups

4 tbsp cilantro, chopped

2 cups basmati rice, cooked

1 package pappadums, prepared as per package directions

METHOD

In a large heavy bottomed pot over medium heat, sauté onions, carrots, garlic, ginger and red pepper in oil. When soft, add curry paste, garam masala, and ground cumin. Add potatoes, yams, galangal root, and lemongrass. Sauté for 5 minutes. Add lime leaves, fish sauce, lime zest and juice, coconut milk and enough stock or water to cover. Simmer until potatoes are tender. Add chickpeas and cook for 10 more minutes. Serve over basmati rice and garnish with fresh cilantro just before serving. Top with crispy pappadums*.

Grilled chicken breast slices would be a great addition to this smooth intensely flavoured curry. And don't forget a spoonful of our Chutney found in the " Sauces" section.

Pappadums can be found at the Kootenay Co-op.

CLINT'S CLAM CHOWDER

Clint from Duncan BC, made the best clam chowder...Clint, your chef's coat is still hanging on your hook!

makes 14-16 bowls

INGREDIENTS

2 white onions or leeks, diced

4 carrots, diced

4 celery stalks, chopped

3 or 4 potatoes, diced

2 cloves garlic, minced

2 bay leaves

3 strips bacon, cut in small pieces

1/4 cup butter

2 tsp thyme

2 tsp tarragon

1 1/2 cups white wine

6 cups fish stock or clam nectar

1 cup whipping cream

1/2 cup flour

1/2 cup oil

2-8 oz cans baby clams, drained

1 tsp Tabasco

juice of 1 lemon

salt and pepper to taste

METHOD

Melt the butter in a large soup pot and sauté onions, carrots, celery, potatoes, garlic, bay leaves and bacon. Cook for about 10 minutes until vegetables are getting soft and fat is rendered from bacon. Add thyme, tarragon, wine, and stock. Simmer for 20 to 30 minutes. Add whipping cream and simmer another 15 minutes. In a small bowl mix together the flour and oil to make a roux. Whisk the roux into the soup to thicken it. Let it come close to a boil, and then turn down the heat to low. Add clams, Tabasco, lemon and season with salt and pepper.

Get out the Saltine crackers!

BROCCOLI AND AGED CHEDDAR SOUP

...Pure comfort food on a frosty winter evening!

serves about 12

INGREDIENTS

2 onions, diced

8 cups broccoli, chopped into small
pieces (to be pureed later so looks
aren't important)

3 tbsp olive oil

3 tbsp butter

8 cups vegetable stock

1 cup heavy cream

1 cup aged cheddar cheese, grated

1 tbsp Worcestershire sauce

1/2 tsp nutmeg

salt and pepper to taste

1/2 cup sherry

1/2 cup parsley

METHOD

In a large soup pot, sauté onions and broccoli in oil and butter. Add stock and simmer until broccoli is tender, about 20 minutes. Puree and return to low heat. Add cream, cheese, Worcestershire sauce, nutmeg, salt and pepper to taste. Simmer for 10-15 more minutes. Turn heat off and whisk in sherry and parsley.

If its not quite thick enough for you, you can always whisk in a little roux made of equal parts of flour and oil, or flour and butter at the end. For this recipe, I would use 1/4 cup of each.

JEFF BRUCE'S **ROASTED** RED **PEPPER** SOUP

Another guaranteed snow bunny pleaser!

serves 12-14

INGREDIENTS

2 tbsp oil

3 leeks, chopped

4 cloves garlic, minced

4 carrots, diced

4 large potatoes, diced

8 cups vegetable stock

1-16 oz jar roasted red peppers
(or 6 whole fresh roasted peppers,
seeds removed)

1-19 oz can tomatoes diced

1 tsp coriander

1 tsp cumin

1 1/2 cups orange juice (fresh
sqeezed is best)

3 tbsp balsamic vinegar

1/2 cup heavy cream (optional)

salt and pepper to taste

1 tsp chipotle paste (optional)

METHOD

In a large soup pot, sauté leeks, garlic, carrots and potatoes in oil. Add stock and simmer until potatoes are soft. Add peppers, tomatoes, spices and orange juice. Simmer 20 minutes and add balsamic vinegar. Purée in food processor and add cream and chipotle paste if using. Salt and pepper to taste.

A wonderful soup- Jeff added zest to our kitchen in so many ways! Slices of baguette topped with goat cheese and broiled for a few minutes are a gorgeous addition – just float on top of the soup!

LEMONY LENTIL SOUP

This lemon and herb flavoured soup tastes fresh and warm on even the coldest day. A great lunch with toasted pita bread and a Greek salad.

serves 8

INGREDIENTS

2 cups red lentils

2 tbsp olive oil

1 large onion, diced

2 tsp salt

6 cloves garlic, minced

3 carrots, diced

1 tsp pepper

1/4 tsp red chili flakes

1 tbsp oregano

1 tbsp fresh rosemary, chopped

2 bay leaves

8 cups vegetable or chicken stock

juice of 2 lemons

2 tsp lemon zest

1 cup feta cheese, crumbled

2 tbsp fresh dill, chopped

METHOD

Rinse the lentils in a colander and set aside to drain. Heat the olive oil in a large pot, add onions and sauté until translucent. Add carrots, garlic, salt, pepper, chili flakes, rosemary, oregano and bay leaves. Stir well and sauté until the carrots are tender. Add the stock and the lentils and bring to a boil. Reduce the heat and simmer for about 25 minutes or until the lentils are soft. Remove the bay leaves, you may puree the soup at this point or leave it just as it is. Add the lemon juice, zest and more salt and pepper to taste. To serve, ladle the soup into bowls and sprinkle the feta and dill on top.

GLORYBOWL

The "Glory Bowl" has become almost as popular as the "Ymir Bowl".
The dressing is truly addictive.

serves 8

INGREDIENTS

THE BOWL
8 cups cooked brown rice
2 cups beets, grated
2 cups carrots, grated
2 cups almonds, toasted
2 cups spinach leaves
2 cups tofu, cubed

GLORY BOWL DRESSING
1/2 cup nutritional yeast flakes*
1/3 cup water
1/3 cup tamari or soy sauce
1/3 cup apple cider vinegar
2 cloves garlic, crushed
1 1/2 cups vegetable oil
2 tbsp tahini paste

METHOD

Prepare your favourite brown rice and set aside. In a skillet sauté tofu cubes. To prepare dressing, combine nutritional yeast flakes, water, tamari or soy sauce, apple cider vinegar, tahini and crushed garlic in blender. Add oil in a steady stream. You will have leftover dressing to use again. To assemble the bowls, place cooked brown rice into 8 bowls, top with beets, carrots, spinach leaves, almonds and sautéed tofu cubes. Drizzle bowls with dressing.

Nutritional yeast flakes can be found at the Kootenay Co-op, or most natural food stores.

So good on any kind of salad greens, spinach, rice, or grains.

SALADS and GREENS

don't forget to eat them everyday

EMMY'S HONEY CURRY SPINACH SALAD

This salad and dressing comes from my talented and hilarious friend
M.E. McKnight, another old pal from my movie catering days.

INGREDIENTS

HONEY CURRY DRESSING (makes 2 cups)

1/2 onion, chopped
1 tsp paprika
1 tsp curry powder
1/2 tsp mustard powder or
1 tsp Dijon mustard
1/2 tsp turmeric
1/2 tsp celery seed
1/2 tsp salt
1/3 cup cider vinegar
1/2 cup honey
1 cup safflower oil

SALAD

1 bag spinach leaves
1/2 cup toasted almonds
1/2 cup red onion, sliced
1 orange peeled and sliced

METHOD

In blender, combine onion, paprika, curry powder, mustard, turmeric, celery seed and salt. Blend well and then add vinegar and honey. In a steady stream, finish with safflower oil. Toss salad with just enough of the dressing to coat spinach. You will have dressing left over for a few more salads!

You can toast the almonds in the oven or in a skillet until they just start to turn brown.

RICE NOODLE SALAD
WITH GRILLED VEGETABLES AND BLACK BEAN VINAIGRETTE

We have used this vinaigrette on several different Whitewater Specials. It is also excellent on grilled salmon or steamed green beans or broccoli!

serves 6-8

INGREDIENTS

RICE NOODLE SALAD
1 package rice noodles
1 eggplant, chopped into
1 inch cubes
1 zucchini, chopped into
1 inch cubes
1 red pepper, chopped into
1 inch cubes
3 tbsp olive oil
1/2 tsp salt
1/2 tsp pepper

BLACK BEAN VINAIGRETTE
2 garlic cloves, minced
1 tbsp fresh ginger, grated
1/2 cup sushi ginger
3 tbsp sushi ginger juice
2 tbsp apple cider vinegar
3/4 tsp salt
3 tbsp sugar
1/4 cup fermented black beans, rinsed
3/4 cup vegetable oil
1 bunch cilantro, chopped
1 bunch green onions, sliced
1/2 cup roasted peanuts, to garnish

METHOD

Roast vegetable cubes in a 350°F oven with salt, pepper and olive oil for 20 minutes. Prepare rice noodles according to package directions. Reserve 2 tsp of black beans. To prepare vinaigrette, combine remaining ingredients, except oil, in blender. Add oil in a steady stream. Then stir in reserved black beans, green onions and cilantro for look and texture. In a bowl, mix noodles with grilled vegetables and dressing, and toss to combine well. Garnish with roasted peanuts.

Grilled prawns make a nice addition to this salad.

*Fermented black beans can be found at Ellison's Market in Nelson.

SPRING GREENS
WITH **MAPLE** BALSAMIC **VINAIGRETTE**

Our "house" salad at home...we eat this at least twice a week! The best spring greens can be found at the Kootenay Co-op.

serves 8

INGREDIENTS

SALAD
12 cups spring greens
1/2 cup crumbled goat cheese
or gorgonzola
3/4 cup pecans, caramelized*
1 cup fresh strawberry slices
or orange slices

VINAIGRETTE
1 tbsp maple syrup
2 tbsp balsamic vinegar
1 tbsp soy sauce
1 clove garlic, crushed
1 tbsp sesame oil
1 tsp pepper
1/2 cup olive oil

METHOD

In large salad bowl, toss spring greens with cheese, pecans and fresh fruit. To prepare the vinaigrette, mix together all ingredients except olive oil until well blended. Add oil in a slow, steady stream until incorporated. Toss greens with dressing.

*To caramelize pecans: spread pecans on baking tray and roast in a 350°F oven until just starting to turn brown. Remove and toss with enough melted butter to lightly coat. Sprinkle nuts with 2 tsp white sugar and 1 tsp salt and toss again. Return to oven for just a few minutes, being careful not to burn them.

SUMMITSALAD
WITH**ROASTED**SUNFLOWER**VINAIGRETTE**

This Pat McInnis inspired salad has been on the menu for years! We keep bringing it back because it's so darn popular!

serves 8

INGREDIENTS

SALAD

8 cups mixed baby salad greens

2 cups beets, grated

2 cups carrots, grated

2 cups chickpeas, drained

2 cups feta cheese, crumbled

2 cups sprouts

1 cup sun-dried tomatoes, sliced

VINAIGRETTE

1 tbsp Dijon mustard

2 tbsp honey

1/2 tsp garlic, crushed

1/2 tsp basil

1 tbsp red wine vinegar

1 tbsp balsamic vinegar

juice and zest of one small orange

3/4 cup safflower oil

1/4 cup roasted sunflower seeds

salt and pepper to taste

METHOD

To prepare the vinaigrette, whisk together Dijon mustard, honey, garlic, basil, red wine vinegar, balsamic vinegar, orange juice and zest. Add oil in a steady stream. Roast sunflower seeds in skillet over medium heat until lightly browned and add to dressing. Season with salt and pepper to taste. On individual salad plates "compose" salads. Starting with the salad greens, then beets, carrots, chickpeas, feta, sprouts and sun dried tomatoes. Spoon dressing over salads.

WARMSPINACHSALAD

Your dinner guests need to be seated before you serve this so that the spinach is just "wilted" when their fork hits the plate!

serves 4-6

INGREDIENTS

3/4 cup olive oil
2 garlic cloves, crushed
1 large shallot, diced
1/3 cup prosciutto, chopped
1/3 cup rice or red wine vinegar
1 cup fresh basil, julienned
1/4 cup pine nuts, toasted
1/4 cup fresh parmesan cheese (or asiago)
salt and freshly ground pepper to taste
10 cups fresh spinach washed and dried

METHOD

Heat the olive oil in large skillet on medium heat. Add garlic, shallots and prosciutto and sauté until shallots are translucent. Add vinegar, salt and pepper. Keep warm. In a large mixing bowl toss the warm vinaigrette with spinach and fresh basil. Top with parmesan cheese and pine nuts.

Many of my close friends are just as passionate about good food as I am. Jann is one of them and this delicious recipe is from her.

TABBOULEH AND CHICKPEA SALAD

A great summer salad and perfect for stuffing pitas!
You'll find this in our deli section.

serves 4-5

INGREDIENTS

SALAD

1 1/2 cups bulgur wheat
1/2 cup red onion, diced
1 cup tomatoes, chopped
1 cup cucumber, chopped
2 tablespoons fresh mint, chopped
2 tablespoons fresh parsley, chopped
1/2 cup pine nuts, toasted
1/2 cup feta cheese, crumbled
1 can chickpeas, drained and rinsed
1/4 cup green olives, sliced

DRESSING

1/4 cup fresh lemon juice and
zest of 1 lemon
1 garlic clove, minced
1/2 tsp oregano
1/2 tsp cumin
1/4 cup red wine vinegar
1 teaspoon Dijon mustard
1/2 cup olive oil
salt and pepper

METHOD

Place bulgur in a bowl and pour 3 cups of boiling water over it. Stir once and let it sit for about 20 minutes or until tender. If there is any water left drain it out in a colander. Add all other salad ingredients to the cooked bulgur and toss to combine well. Whisk together dressing ingredients and season to taste with salt and pepper. Pour the dressing over the salad and toss well.

ASIAN SLAW

This "coleslaw" is great alone or as part of our popular "Shanghai Wrap" located in the "Savouries" section.

makes 5 cups

INGREDIENTS

2 cups green cabbage, shredded

2 cups red cabbage, shredded

1 cup carrots, shredded

1/2 cup cilantro, chopped

1/2 cup green onions, chopped

1 tbsp toasted sesame seeds

METHOD

Combine all ingredients in a large mixing bowl and toss with about 1 cup Glory Bowl Salad Dressing.

Glory Bowl Salad Dressing is found in the "Soups and Bowls" section.

POTATO SALAD **WITH** MUSTARD **DILL** DRESSING

A real hit of mustard and just right with any of our sandwiches.

serves 6

INGREDIENTS

1 1/2 pounds red new potatoes
1/4 cup Dijon mustard
1/8 cup grainy mustard
1/2 cup olive oil
1 tbsp balsamic or sherry vinegar
1/4 cup minced onion
3 tbsp chopped fresh dill
salt and pepper to taste

METHOD

Bring a large pot of salted water to a boil. Dice the potatoes and cook them in the water till tender but not mushy! Drain. Mix together all remaining ingredients and toss with the still warm potatoes. Serve this salad slightly warm or at room temperature.

PETRA'S QUINOA AND BLACK BEAN SALAD

This recipe came from a good friend who loves great tasting and super healthy food. Quinoa is a South American high protein grain found in any health food store.

INGREDIENTS

1 cup raw quinoa
1 tbsp olive oil
1 tsp paprika
2 cups water
1 tsp salt
1 cup black beans, cooked
2 cups corn
2 tbsp olive oil
1 large onion, finely chopped (about 2 cups)
2 garlic cloves, minced

1 tsp ground cumin
1 tsp ground coriander
2 red peppers, diced
1 large tomato, diced
1 fresh chile, chopped very finely
2 tbsp parsley, chopped
2 tsp cilantro, chopped
1/4 cup fresh lemon juice
salt and pepper to taste

METHOD

In a sieve, rinse the quinoa under running water and set aside to drain. Heat the oil in a saucepan, add paprika and stir constantly for about 1 minute. Add the quinoa, 2 cups water and salt. Cover and bring to a boil. Lower the heat and simmer for 15-20 minutes, or until the water is absorbed and the quinoa is tender but still a tiny bit chewy. In a skillet, heat oil and sauté the onions, garlic, cumin and coriander until onions are translucent. Stir in red peppers, chile and cilantro. Sauté for another 5 minutes. In a large bowl, combine the quinoa and sautéed vegetables and chill for 15 minutes. Stir in the corn, black beans, tomatoes, parsley, lemon juice, salt and pepper.

Toasted pine nuts, green olives and feta cheese all make great additions to this salad.

KID'S CAESAR SALAD

This is not your spicy, garlicky, bold in your face type of Caesar salad.
This is what the kid's like, mild and creamy, lots of crunchy croutons, fresh romaine lettuce and good Parmesan cheese. This salad makes everyone happy, even the pickiest eaters. Our thanks to Christina for sharing this one.

serves 6

INGREDIENTS

DRESSING
1 egg
juice of 1/2 lemon
1 clove garlic
1 tsp anchovy paste
pinch of sugar
1/2 tsp salt
1/2 tsp pepper
1/2 cup to 3/4 cup vegetable oil or olive oil (I use some of both)

SALAD
1 large head of romaine lettuce cleaned and chopped
1/2 cup freshly grated Parmesan cheese
1 1/2 cups croutons

METHOD

Put all dressing ingredients except oil, in a blender and combine well. Add oil in a steady stream. Taste for salt and pepper. This makes about a cup of dressing. Add the dressing to the cleaned and chopped lettuce. Toss in the Parmesan cheese and croutons.

To make croutons - toss cubed bread in some olive oil, salt, pepper and some minced garlic. Toast on a cookie sheet in a 300°F oven till golden brown and crispy.

Add some grilled boneless chicken slices for a quick midweek meal. If you are concerned about using a raw egg, you can use 1/2 cup mayonnaise instead.

GRILLED FRESH ARTICHOKES

When I was a kid growing up in West Vancouver, my Mom grew beautiful artichokes in our garden. They were so tall she needed a ladder to cut them off the stalk!

serves 4

INGREDIENTS

2 fresh artichokes
1/2 cup olive oil
juice of 1 lemon
1/2 cup fresh mint, chopped

METHOD

To prepare artichokes, cut off the base and remove about one-third of the bottom outer leaves. Trim the artichokes pointed end, cutting off about the top 1/4 inch. Cut artichokes in half and remove and discard the fluffy pink middle. Rub immediately with lemon juice to prevent browning. Bring a large pot of water to boil. Drop in the artichokes. Cover and boil for about 20 minutes or until tender. Check to see if they are cooked by pulling on 1 or 2 leaves – if they pull out easily the artichokes are cooked - if you have to tug, let them boil for another 5 minutes. Remove the artichokes, drain and place in a bowl. Combine olive oil, mint and lemon and pour over cooked artichokes. You can prepare these well ahead and let them marinate until it's time to turn on the grill. Grill artichokes on a medium hot barbeque until grill marks appear on both sides, about 8 minutes. Serve warm or at room temperature with Garlic Aioli found in our "Sauces" section, or with a simple garlic butter.

Artichokes are the most sensuous things to share with someone you love...

SAVOURIES

to keep you warm out there in the snow!

WHITEWATERVEGGIEBURGER

Developed by Pat McInnis of Alligator Pie Catering. If you or anyone you love is a veggie burger fan, you will want to have a stash of these in your freezer at all times. Make them once and you'll never be satisfied with anything you can buy in the grocery store.
A food processor will come in handy here.

makes 12 burgers

INGREDIENTS

1 tbsp vegetable oil
1 onion, diced
1 clove garlic, minced
1 tbsp cumin
1 1/2 tbsp chili powder
1-19 oz can black beans, drained, rinsed and roughly pureed
1 tsp oregano
1/4 cup parsley or cilantro, chopped

2 tbsp sesame oil
1/2 cup almonds, roasted and chopped
1 cup sunflower seeds, roasted and chopped
3 cups fine bread crumbs
1/2 cup soy sauce
5 eggs
2 cups carrots, grated
2 cups oats
flour for dredging
2 tbsp vegetable oil

METHOD

In a large skillet, sauté onions and garlic in oil. Place in large mixing bowl and let it cool a little. Add remaining ingredients. Mix well and shape into patties. Dredge lightly in flour. Heat vegetable oil in a large pan to brown the burgers on both sides, you may need to do this in batches with a bit more oil.

We serve our Veggie Burgers on Johnny's Bakery whole-wheat burger buns topped with fresh local "Glade Farm" Daikon sprouts and Roasted Garlic Aioli or Tzatziki, both found in the "Sauces" section.

PANINIS

Not really a "recipe", but three great combinations that we use on our popular grilled sandwiches called "Paninis".

INGREDIENTS

THE "TUSCAN"
focaccia bread
pesto (store bought is fine)
grilled and sliced Chorizo sausage
provolone cheese
caramelized onions
arugula or spinach

THE "SICILLIAN"
focaccia bread
pesto (store bought is fine)
goat cheese and cream cheese
(equal parts mixed together)
roasted red peppers
artichoke hearts
provolone cheese
arugula or spinach

THE "BAMBINI"
focaccia bread
cooked bacon
cheddar cheese

METHOD

Assemble sandwiches. Brush with olive oil and grill until the cheese melts. Panini makers and sandwich grills are available at all price ranges these days, but you can get similar results with a good frying pan and something heavy to weigh down the top of the sandwich while it cooks.

SHANGHAIWRAP

A new wrap on the menu, developed by local caterer and one of my oldest and dearest cooking partners Joanne Ryan.

serves 12

INGREDIENTS

DRY RUB
1-4 or 5 lb pork shoulder
or pork butt roast
1/3 cup sugar
1 tbsp garlic powder
1 1/2 tsp paprika
1 tbsp seasoning salt
1 tbsp onion powder

BBQ SAUCE
1 medium onion, diced
2 cloves garlic, minced
1 1/2 tsp fresh ginger, minced
4 oz hoisin sauce
1 cup cider vinegar
1 1/2 tbsp Worcestershire sauce
3 tbsp sesame oil

1/2 cup honey
1/2 cup soy sauce
1 small can tomato paste
1 1/2 tsp Chinese 5-spice powder
1/2 tsp cayenne
tortillas, or
sub-type buns

METHOD

Combine all ingredients for dry rub and apply to pork roast. BBQ or cook roast in 350°F oven for 2 hours or until juice runs clear. When cool enough to handle, shred the pork, (a fork and your hands work best here.) You may want to discard some of the fattier bits from the meat. To prepare BBQ sauce, sauté onion, garlic and ginger until soft. Add hoisin sauce, vinegar, Worcestershire sauce, sesame oil, honey, soy sauce, tomato paste, Chinese 5-spice and cayenne. Simmer for 20 minutes. To assemble wrap, mix pork with BBQ sauce. Wrap in tortilla or a fresh sub-type bun and stuff with Asian Slaw found in the "Salads and Bowls" section.

The Pork and Barbeque Sauce can be frozen in small bags and reheated as needed...

RUNAWAY TRAIN WRAP

This has been a very popular wrap and is a quick, easy meal to prepare when you have a house full of hungry teenagers and some leftover chicken in the fridge.

serves 6

INGREDIENTS

3 boneless chicken breasts, cooked and sliced
6 tomato tortillas
2 onions, caramelized*
3/4 cup Runaway Train BBQ Sauce**
1 cup Roasted Corn Salsa
1 cup lettuce, shredded

METHOD

In a skillet, sauté chicken until just heated. Remove from pan and set aside. In the same pan, place tortilla to quickly heat up. To assemble the wrap, place tortilla on work space and spread chicken, caramelized onions, BBQ sauce, salsa and lettuce. Roll up and slice in half.

*To caramelize onions: In a skillet, place sliced onions and sauté in oil until translucent. Add 1 tbsp brown sugar and 1 tbsp balsamic vinegar per onion. Cook at low heat for another 15-20 minutes until "syrupy" looking. Season with salt and pepper.

Roasted Corn Salsa can be found in the "Sauces" section.

**Runaway Train BBQ Sauce made by Cherry Bomb Productions can be found in several locations in Nelson.

FRESH TRACKS

* comes with soup or fries

...AWAY TRAIN WRAP

...hicken or Silverking tofu,
...zed onions, roasted corn, red pepper,
...nd Runaway Train BBQ
...on a tomato tortilla $7⁹⁵

*   *   *

...C SALMON ROLL *

...salmon, dilled cream cheese,
...and summit greens & red onions *
...ed in warm Pita *

...ANGI...

shredded ti...
& sesame -...
on a fresh...
$8⁵⁰

SAMOSA...

served wit...
& tzatziki
$6²⁵

VEGETARIAN BLACK BEAN CHILI

This is what you want to make when all the relatives are coming to town for a ski holiday and you'd like to be able to get a few runs in too! Make it a day or 2 ahead - the flavours just get better. You will need a big pot, at least 8 quarts.

feeds about 12 hungry skiers

INGREDIENTS

1/4 cup oil
2 onions, diced
6 carrots, diced
6 stalks of celery, diced
2 zucchinis, diced
1 jalapeno pepper, minced finely
1 tbsp garlic, minced
1/4 cup chili powder
2 tsp ground cumin
2 tsp basil
2 tsp oregano
2 bay leaves

2 tsp salt
1-19 oz.can chickpeas, drained and rinsed
1 can kidney beans, drained and rinsed
2 cups corn frozen or fresh
2 cans cooked black beans, drained and rinsed
2-28 fl. oz. cans diced tomatoes
1 bottle of Nelson Brewing Company Beer*
1 tsp chipotle in adobo paste,
found at Ellison's in a can
water or stock
1 bunch cilantro, chopped
2 or 3 limes

METHOD

In a large pot, sauté onions, carrots, celery, zucchini, jalapeno pepper and garlic in oil until soft. Add chili powder, ground cumin, basil, oregano, salt and bay leaves. Sauté 2-3 minutes more, then add chickpeas, kidney beans, black beans, corn, tomatoes, beer and chipotle paste. Add water or stock to cover and let simmer for about an hour stirring often Add 1 bunch of cilantro, juice and zest of 3 limes and salt and pepper to taste.

Serve with Fresh Tracks Corn Bread.

*"The Nelson Brewing Company" originally established in 1897 and revived in 1992 to become the West Kootenay's premier beer maker.

Saute
4   onions, in hot oil, then add
6   carrots
1 tbsp   garlic
1 tbsp   ginger
3   red peppers, add last

SPANAKOPITA

Spanakopitas sell out everyday, people can't believe they're available at 5,400 feet! Serve with Tzatziki.

makes about 24 triangles

INGREDIENTS

1 large onion, diced
1/4 cup olive oil
1 tbsp dill
1 tbsp oregano
2 tbsp garlic, minced
1/2 tsp mint
1/2 cup white wine

2 packages frozen spinach, thawed, drained and chopped
2 cups feta cheese, crumbled
2 eggs
1/4 cup fresh lemon juice
1 pack phyllo pastry
1/2 cup melted butter

METHOD

In a large skillet, sauté onions in olive oil. Add dill, oregano, garlic and mint. Sauté 3-4 minutes more and then add wine. Cook until wine has reduced. Remove from heat and let cool a little before adding spinach, cheese, eggs and lemon juice. Combine well. Make a stack of 4 sheets of phyllo pastry, brushing each layer with melted butter. Cut into 4 equal strips. Work with 1 strip of phyllo at a time. Cover remaining phyllo in tea towel. Lay strip down in front of you. Spoon 2 heaping tablespoons of filling in bottom corner of strip and fold in half diagonally, creating a triangle. Continue folding over into triangular shape until you reach end of strip. Repeat until all filling is used up. Brush tops with a little more butter. Place triangles on baking sheet and bake in a 350°F oven for 20-25 minutes, or until golden brown.

This is a fairly large recipe so freeze some for later. If cooking previously frozen spinach triangles, don't let them thaw first – straight from freezer to oven.

CHILI BLACK **BEAN** SAUCE **FOR** CHICKEN **WINGS**

On the Bar Menu for many years – these wings are best deep fried, but a hot oven works well here too. Have a cold Nelson Brewing Company beer nearby!

serves 10-12

INGREDIENTS

5 lbs chicken wings
1/2 cup Louisiana Hot Sauce
2 tbsp fermented black beans, well rinsed
3 tbsp brown sugar
1 tbsp Worcestershire sauce
1 tsp Dijon mustard
2 tbsp sweet soy sauce
zest and juice of 2 limes
zest and juice of 1/2 orange

METHOD

Line a large roasting pan with foil and coat it with a little oil. Bake wings in hot 400°F oven for 40 minutes or until crispy, drain off fat. Let cool. In a mixing bowl, combine the remaining ingredients. Pour sauce over wings and toss until well coated. Return to hot oven in covered roasting pan for 15-20 minutes.

Serve with cilantro and lime wedges. You might want to tone down the Louisiana a little bit if small children are involved.

SAMOSAS

We've had these on the menu for many years and although they're fiddly to make, people go wild for them! We used to deep-fry them, but people in the Kootenays are so darn healthy...we oven bake them now and they sell like "hot (healthy) cakes"! We owe our kudos to Pat McInnis and Cathy Crooks.

makes approximately 12-16

INGREDIENTS

DOUGH

3 cups flour
1/2 tsp salt
1/2 tsp baking powder
1/4 tsp turmeric
1/4 tsp paprika
2/3 cup cold butter, cubed
2/3 cup cold water

FILLING

1 tbsp oil
1 cup onions, diced
1 tbsp ginger, minced
1 tbsp garlic, minced
2 tsp cumin
2 tsp curry powder
1 1/2 tsp coriander
1 tsp turmeric
2 tsp chili sauce
1/4 cup lemon juice
1/2 cup unsweetened coconut milk
5 cups potatoes, cubed in 1/2 inch pieces
1/2 head cauliflower, chopped into small pieces
1 cup frozen peas
1/2 bunch cilantro, chopped
2 tsp salt

METHOD

Place flour, salt, baking powder, turmeric and paprika into food processor. Add butter and process until sand-like, approximately 10 seconds. Add water and pulse until mixture just comes together. Wrap dough in saran wrap and allow it to rest in fridge for at least an hour. Boil potato and cauliflower pieces until tender. In a large skillet, sauté onion, ginger and garlic until tender. Add spices and cook for one minute. Over medium heat add remaining filling ingredients except the peas and cook for about 4 to 5 minutes until mixture is well combined. Fold in peas and adjust seasoning. Let the filling cool. On a lightly floured surface, roll out dough and use a "sour cream" or "yogurt" type lid (5 inches in diameter) to cut shape. Place approximately 1/4 cup of filling on half of the circle of dough. Fold the dough over to make a half-moon. Seal the edges well by pinching the dough together. Place the samosas on a lightly oiled cookie sheet. Brush with an egg wash. Bake in a 350°F oven for approximately 30 minutes, or shallow-fry them in 1 1/2" - 2" vegetable oil until golden brown.

Homemade Mango Chutney found in our "Sauces" section is what we serve them with, but"Major Grey's' is always good too.

MOROCCAN CHICKEN PHYLLO PIE

Another recipe from the amazing Val Grlic...serve this with the Spring Green Salad with Maple Balsamic Dressing found in the "Salads" section.

serves 8-10

INGREDIENTS

3 tbsp vegetable oil

1 onion, finely chopped

1 garlic clove, chopped

3 whole boneless, skinless chicken breasts, diced

1 tsp ground cumin

1 tsp ground cinnamon

1 tsp harissa (optional)

2 tsp tomato paste

2 tsp honey

4 tbsp lemon juice

1/4 cup blanched almonds, finely chopped

1 1/2 cups dried fruit soaked for several hours in 1/2 cup boiling water (apricots, mangoes, prunes, papayas...)

8 sheets phyllo pastry

1/2 cup melted butter

METHOD

In a large skillet, sauté onion and garlic in oil. When onions are transparent, add chicken pieces and cook until browned. Add cumin and cinnamon and sauté for 2 minutes. Stir in harisssa, tomato paste, honey and lemon juice. Cook for another 5 minutes, then add chopped almonds and dried fruit. Season with salt and pepper. Place phyllo pastry in a spring form pan 1 sheet at a time brushing each layer with butter, letting the excess pastry hang over the edge. Pour the slightly cooled chicken mixture into the prepared pan. Fold over the sides of the phyllo pastry and top the pan with the two remaining sheets of phyllo, which have also been brushed with butter. Bake in a 350°F oven for about 40 minutes, or until golden brown.

Any chutney, salsa or yogurt based sauce would suit this crispy, flavourful creation.

WEST COAST CRAB CAKES

This one is for my mother Bernice who will do almost anything to get her hands on some fresh crab! We make this for a lunch special on Valentine's Day or Magic Mondays.

serves 4

INGREDIENTS

1 lb Dungeness crab*
1 cup fresh bread crumbs
1/3 cup green onions, diced
1 red pepper, diced
4 tbsp mayonnaise
salt and pepper to taste
vegetable oil for frying
1/4 cup fresh chopped cilantro or basil

METHOD

In a large mixing bowl combine all ingredients. Form into patties. In a skillet, fry the patties in vegetable oil approximately 4-5 minutes on each side.

Simple and light, serve with our Sun-Dried Tomato & Fennel Chutney found in the "Sauces" section.

*Dungeness crab can be found at Nelson's "The Fish Market" on Ward St.

TORTARUSTICA
WITH TOMATO-CHIPOTLE SAUCE AND LEMON-BASIL AIOLI

I created this for my incredible dad, Ron, who shared with me his love of travel and sailing and eating food in beautiful locations.

serves 12

INGREDIENTS

1 package 10 inch flour tortillas*
1 cup pesto, store bought is fine
8 oz goat cheese
3 cups mozzarella cheese, grated
1 eggplant
2 zucchinis
2 red peppers
2 yellow peppers
2 yams
2 potatoes

2 red onions
1/4 cup olive oil
1 tbsp rosemary
(fresh if possible)

LEMON-BASIL AIOLI

1 cup mayonnaise
juice of 1 lemon
1/2 cup fresh basil, chopped

TOMATO-CHIPOTLE SAUCE

10 tomatoes, quartered
1 red onion, large dice
3 garlic cloves
1/4 cup olive oil
1 tbsp brown sugar
1 tsp chipotle in adobo paste
1/4 cup cilantro, chopped

METHOD

Slice all vegetables in similar widths and toss with olive oil and rosemary. Grill or roast in a 350°F oven until soft, approx. 20 minutes. Prepare the rest of the torta ingredients. To assemble: Start making layers in springform pan. You will be making a layered torta using 1 type of roasted vegetable and some of each cheese and a little of the pesto between each tortilla every layer. Rub top with olive oil and more mozzarella and cover with tin foil. Put in a 350°F oven and bake for 50-60 minutes.

To prepare tomato sauce, toss tomatoes, onion and garlic with olive oil and brown sugar. Roast in a 350°F oven for 30 minutes or until caramelized. Puree in food processor and then add chipotle and cilantro. To prepare aioli, mix all ingredients together. To serve, spoon some of the warm sauce on a plate, set a slice of torta on top and drizzle with basil aioli.

This is a bit of a project (but well worth it), so assemble the torta and the sauces one day ahead and bake it the day of your party.
* We like to use a combination of red and green tortillas.

PADTHAI**FRIED**NOODLES

When we serve this as a special at the mountain, we make a giant amount of it in the morning, cool it, then reheat portions as it's ordered. If making at home have everything ready to go and serve right away.

serves 6

INGREDIENTS

16 oz package of rice noodles

1/2 cup vegetable oil

5 garlic cloves, finely chopped

1 lb cooked shrimp

1/4 cup pickled radish, chopped (available at "Wings Grocery" on Baker Street)

1 package tofu, cut into 1/2 inch cubes

1/2 cup white vinegar

1/4 cup fish sauce

2 tbsp ketchup

1/4 cup sugar

2 eggs, beaten

1/4 lb bean sprouts

3 green onions, sliced

1/4 cup roasted peanuts

cilantro for garnish

1 lime, cut into wedges

METHOD

Cook rice noodles according to package directions. In a large skillet, heat oil and fry garlic until golden. Add shrimp, radish and tofu. Cook 3-5 minutes. Set aside in separate dish. Reheat skillet and add vinegar, ketchup, fish sauce and sugar. Heat well and add noodles. When noodles are completely coated, spread them to the sides of the pan and scramble eggs in the middle. Fold noodles over the eggs. Add shrimp, tofu, radish, green onions and bean sprouts. Serve on a large platter and garnish with peanuts, cilantro, and lime wedges.

My daughter Ali goes wild for these noodles. We use locally made "Silverking Tofu" in all our recipes that call for tofu.

SRI LANKAN CHICKEN CURRY

This is an extremely popular lunch special served over basmati rice with a spoonful of our homemade Mango Chutney, Raita and crispy pappadums.

serves 8-10

INGREDIENTS

3 tbsp oil
1/4 tsp fenugreek seeds
10 lime leaves
2 large onions, chopped
2 cloves garlic, finely chopped
4 tsp ginger, chopped
1 tsp turmeric
1 tsp ground coriander
1 tsp ground cumin
3/4 tsp ground fennel

2 tsp red paprika
2 tsp salt
2 tbsp vinegar
3 lb boneless chicken breast or thigh meat, cubed
3 tomatoes, chopped
6 cardamom pods
1 stick cinnamon
2 large strips lemon rind
1 cup coconut milk

METHOD

In a large skillet, heat oil and quickly toast fenugreek seeds and lime leaves. Add onions, garlic and ginger. Sauté until soft. Add ground spices, salt and vinegar. Stir well. Add chicken and coat with spices by stirring. Add tomatoes, whole spices and lemon rind. Cook covered over low heat for 30 minutes. Remove whole spices and lemon rind if possible. Add coconut milk and salt. Cook for only 5-10 minutes more.

I carried this curry in my pack up to the Kokanee Glacier cabin to feed a group of my girlfriends last summer, we loved it and you'll see it on next year's menu.

LOVELY'S ASIAN STYLE RISOTTO

This recipe comes from my friend Linda and is so named because everything she makes is just "lovely".

serves 4

INGREDIENTS

CHILI-GARLIC DRIZZLE
2 tbsp sesame oil
1 jalapeno chili pepper, very finely chopped and seeded
1 garlic clove, chopped
4 tbsp soy sauce
2 tbsp rice wine vinegar
1 tbsp sugar

RISOTTO
2 tbsp olive oil
1 cup onions, chopped
1 cup pancetta (Italian cured bacon), diced
1 cup shiitake mushrooms, sliced
1 cup Arborio rice
1 cup white wine
3 cups hot chicken stock (more or less)
3 tbsp butter
1/2 cup fresh cilantro, chopped
1 cup spicy greens or fresh spinach, loosely chopped
1 cup parmesan cheese, freshly grated

METHOD

To prepare the chili-garlic drizzle, heat sesame oil in a small pan and sauté chili pepper and garlic until fragrant. Remove from heat and add the soy, vinegar and sugar. Set aside. In a large pot, sauté onions in olive oil until softened. Add the pancetta and mushrooms and sauté until slightly browned. Add the rice and keep stirring until golden. Add wine and keep simmering and stirring adding the hot stock 1/2 cup at a time until risotto is creamy. Stir in butter. When you are ready to serve, add fresh cilantro, greens, parmesan and mix together lightly. The greens should be just wilted. Spoon your reserved chili-garlic drizzle over the plated Risotto and serve with more parmesan cheese.

Serve with Tuna and Wasabi Lime Sauce or Thai Marinated Lamb – both recipes can be found in this section.

STICKY 5 SPICE RIBS

Served in Coal-Oil Johnny's Bar at Whitewater. These are delicious cut up small as an appetizer, or left in racks for a dinner.

serves 4-6 as an appetizer

INGREDIENTS

4 lbs baby back ribs
4 tbsp rice wine vinegar
2 tbsp brown sugar
2 tbsp oyster sauce
1 tsp Chinese 5-spice powder
2 clove garlic minced
1 cup hoisin sauce

METHOD

Cut ribs into serving size and place in a heavy-duty zip lock bag or sealable container. Mix together all remaining ingredients and pour over ribs coating them well. Marinate in the refrigerator for at least 4 hours or up to 24 hours, turning occasionally. Transfer ribs and marinade to a foil-lined baking pan and roast uncovered in a hot 400°F oven for 10 minutes. Turn down oven to 300°F and continue roasting for 40-50 minutes, turning and basting occasionally.

You'll need a finger bowl nearby and an icy cold Nelson Brewing Company beer!

GREEK LAMB BURGERS

A yummy alternative to regular beef burgers.
These are a big hit on a snowy day.

makes 12-1/4 lb burgers

INGREDIENTS

3 lbs ground lamb
6 cloves garlic, roasted and mashed*
1 tsp ground cinnamon
1 tsp ground allspice
1 1/2 tbsp fresh oregano, if available or
 dried whole oregano leaves

2 eggs, lightly beaten
1 tsp salt
1 tsp pepper
4 tbsp coarse bread crumbs

METHOD

In a large mixing bowl, mix together lamb, roasted garlic, cinnamon, allspice and oregano. Add eggs to the meat mixture and combine well. Add salt, pepper and bread crumbs. Form into 12 patties. Grill just like a regular burger.

*To roast garlic, wrap head in foil paper and roast in a 350°F oven for 35-40 minutes, or until garlic is soft. Remove from foil and squeeze out garlic.

We serve our Lamb Burgers on a kaiser bun with Eggplant Spread, Tzatziki, crumbled feta and fresh spinach leaves. Eggplant Spread and Tzatziki Spread can both be found in the "Sauces" section.

INDIANCHICKENBURGER

Another burger alternative – after all it is a ski resort cafeteria!

makes 8 burgers

INGREDIENTS

2 lbs ground chicken
2 garlic cloves, minced
2 eggs, lightly beaten
1 tsp curry powder
2 tsp garam masala
1 cup fine dry bread crumbs
1 tsp salt
1 tsp pepper

METHOD

Place chicken, garlic, eggs, curry powder, garam masala, salt, pepper and bread crumbs in a large mixing bowl. Combine well. Shape into 8 patties. They will feel stickier then regular burgers. Brush with vegetable oil and grill for 5-6 minutes per side. Serve on a fresh hamburger bun with Mango Chutney, Raita, cucumber and tomato slices.

Mango Chutney and Raita can be found in the "Sauces" section.

AHI TUNA **WITH** WASABI **LIME** SAUCE

Here's something that is not on the menu but a special treat we make at home with tuna or halibut or the best fresh fish we can afford. A simple preparation for the fish, and a really delicious sauce.

serves 4

INGREDIENTS

TUNA
6 oz ahi tuna fillets, 1 per person
2 tsp fresh dill, chopped
2 tsp oil

SAUCE
1/2 cup soy sauce
1/4 cup lime juice
1 tsp wasabi paste
8 tbsp cold butter cut into small pieces
1/4 cup green onions, chopped
1/4 cup cilantro, chopped

METHOD

Brush tuna with oil and dill. Cook on a medium-high barbeque or in a skillet approximately 3 minutes per side. To prepare sauce, combine soy sauce and lime juice in a saucepan. Let reduce for 10 minutes. Whisk in wasabi paste and then the cold butter bit by bit until incorporated. Just before serving, stir in green onions and cilantro. Drizzle over fish.

Serve with Lovely's Asian Risotto found in this section.

CHICKEN MARBELLA

This is a great "Skier's Dish" because you make it all the day ahead. Get home from the slopes at 5:00 and stick it in the oven. Serve with rice and a green salad with Glory Bowl Dressing...SO GOOD!

serves 6-8

INGREDIENTS

5 lbs chicken pieces, legs and thighs are best

6 cloves garlic

1 tbsp dried oregano

2 tsp salt

2 tsp pepper

1/4 cup red wine vinegar

1/4 cup olive oil

1/2 cup pitted prunes, chopped in small pieces

1/2 cup dried figs, chopped in quarters

1/4 cup Spanish green olives, pitted and whole

1/4 cup capers with a bit of juice

3 bay leaves

1/2 cup brown sugar

1 cup white wine

2 tbsp parsley, chopped

METHOD

Combine all ingredients except parsley and marinate chicken pieces overnight, turning occasionally. This overnight marination is essential to the moistness and flavour of the dish. Arrange chicken pieces in a large shallow baking pan and pour marinade over. Bake in a 350°F oven for 50 minutes, basting frequently with the pan juices. When done it should be a nice deep golden brown colour. Sprinkle with parsley.

Right out of the oven or at room temperature this is a great dish for a crowd and pure comfort food on a cold, winter day. Glory Bowl Dressing is located in our "Soups and Bowls" section.

THAI MARINADE **FOR** LAMB **OR** CHICKEN

This is one of our all time favourites. Great for almost any cut of meat.
Try it once and it will be part of your repertoire forever!

INGREDIENTS

2 tbsp red curry paste

3 tbsp garlic, minced

1 tsp curry powder

1 tbsp ginger, diced

1 tsp fresh mint, chopped or 1/2 tsp
dried mint

2 tbsp cilantro, chopped

1 tbsp lemon grass, chopped or lemon zest

1 tbsp sugar

3 tbsp fish sauce

3 tbsp olive oil

1/2 tsp pepper

14 oz coconut milk

METHOD

Mix together all ingredients. Place your lamb or chicken in a heavy duty zip-lock bag or other air tight container and pour marinade over. Make sure meat is well coated with the marinade. Seal it up and refrigerate overnight or for at least 6 hours. Roast in a 350°F oven or barbeque on a medium low grill. Cooking times noted below.

Serve with Lovely's Asian Style Risotto, also found in this section.

One whole 3-4 lb chicken will take about 1 hour. A thermometer inserted in the thickest part of the thigh should read 160-165°F.

One 3-4 lb butterflied leg of lamb will take about 35 minutes depending on your preference for doneness. A thermometer inserted in the thickest part should read about 125°F.

2 racks of lamb about 2 lbs per rack will take about 30 minutes. 2 rib racks will feed 4-5 people.

CHILICON CARNE

My son Conner's favourite lunch on a big powder day.
He likes it heaped on a mountain of french fries of course.

INGREDIENTS

2 tbsp vegetable oil

1 large onion, diced

4 cloves garlic, minced

1/2 bunch celery, diced

2 green peppers, diced

2 1/2 lbs ground beef

2 tbsp chili powder

1 tbsp cumin

2 tsp pepper

2 tsp salt

2 tsp onion powder

1-28 oz. can kidney beans

2-28 oz. cans diced tomatoes

1 small tin tomato paste

1/4 cup brown sugar

1/4 cup apple cider vinegar

METHOD

Heat the oil in a large pot and cook the meat until browned, drain the meat into a colander over a bowl and set aside. Using the same pot (you may need a little more oil) sauté the onion for a couple of minutes. Add garlic, celery, and green peppers and sauté for 5-8 minutes more. Then add the chili powder, cumin, onion powder, salt and pepper, stirring to combine well. Add the beef to the vegetables and all the remaining ingredients: kidney beans, tomatoes, tomato paste, brown sugar and cider vinegar. Bring to a boil, turn down the heat and simmer for 1 hour.

We serve this in big bowls topped with grated cheddar cheese, or as the previously mentioned "Chili fries." (It's a teenage boy thing). This chili is also wrapped up in a flour tortilla with grated cheese and rice, and topped with sour cream, black olives, green onions, and salsa to make our ever popular Beef Burrito.

PASTA WITH SHIITAKE MUSHROOMS PROSCIUTTO AND TOMATOES

Nothing like a big plate of pasta to warm you up between runs!

serves 8-10

INGREDIENTS

4 cups bow-tie, or farfalle shaped pasta

2 cups onions, diced

2 garlic cloves, minced

1/4 tsp dried chilies

2 tbsp olive oil

1 tsp dried or fresh basil

1 tsp oregano

1 lb shiitake mushrooms, sliced thinly

1/4 cup butter

3 tbsp flour

2 cups milk

2-20 oz tins canned diced Italian tomatoes, drained

1/4 lb prosciutto, thinly sliced

1/4 lb fontina cheese, grated

1/4 lb gorgonzola cheese, crumbled

1 1/2 cups parmesan cheese

2/3 cup parsley, chopped

1/2 cup toasted pine nuts

METHOD

In a large pot, cook pasta until al dente in salted, boiling water. Drain and set aside. Meanwhile, in a large skillet sauté onions, garlic and chilies in olive oil. Add basil, oregano and shiitake mushrooms. Sauté for 5 minutes. In a separate pot, melt butter and whisk in flour. Add milk and heat until thickened. Turn heat to low and add tomatoes. In large bowl, combine pasta, sautéed onions, mushrooms, white sauce, prosciutto, cheeses and parsley. Mix together and transfer to a baking dish and sprinkle with toasted pine nuts. Cover and bake in a 350°F oven for 30 minutes.

Rich and fulfilling! Can be made day before and reheated in oven... Bon Appetit!

BAKED PHYLLO SPRING ROLLS
WITH CHILI-LIME PEANUT DIPPING SAUCE

Crunchy and light, these pork or tofu filled rolls are a big hit in Coal Oil Johnny's Bar or at any party…

makes 16 to 24 rolls

INGREDIENTS

SPRING ROLLS

1/2 lb pork sausage or mild Italian sausage or
1/2 lb tofu, grated
2 cups fennel bulb, finely chopped
1 cup onion, finely chopped
1 carrot, grated
2 tbsp ginger, minced
2 tbsp garlic, minced

1/2 tsp fennel seed
2 tbsp oil
2 tbsp sesame oil
1 tbsp hoisin sauce
1/2 tsp Chinese 5-spice powder
8 to 12 sheets phyllo pastry
1/2 cup butter

DIPPING SAUCE

1/3 cup sweet soy sauce (available at Ellison's Market in Nelson)
2 tbsp sweet chili sauce
2 tbsp roasted peanuts, crushed
2 tbsp chopped cilantro
2 tbsp lime juice

METHOD

In a large skillet with a little oil, sauté pork or tofu until cooked. Drain and set aside. In the same pan, sauté fennel, onion, carrot, garlic, ginger and fennel seed in oils. When soft, add pork or tofu, hoisin sauce and chinese-5-spice. To prepare the spring rolls, make a stack of 4 sheets of phyllo, brushing each layer with melted butter. Cut in half width-wise and then into 4 length-wise pieces giving you 8 rectangles. Put approximately 2 tbsp filling on each square and roll up "jelly-roll" fashion, tucking ends in to seal. Repeat with remaining 4 sheets of phyllo . When all filling is used up, place rolls on baking sheet and bake in a 350°F oven for approximately 25 minutes. To prepare dipping sauce, mix together all ingredients in a small mixing bowl.

Can be frozen before cooking on layers of wax paper in Tupperware type containers. If frozen make sure the rolls go straight from the freezer to the oven, otherwise the filling can seep out through the pastry. A great make ahead appetizer…

ROASTED VEGETABLE STRUDEL
WITH BALSAMIC REDUCTION

A beautiful Magic Monday special made by Val Grlic. A great light lunch accompanied by a green salad with goat cheese, strawberries, and pecans.

serves 6-8

INGREDIENTS

3 tbsp olive oil
2 red peppers, cubed
1 eggplant, cubed
1 zucchini, cubed
1 red onion, cubed
1 cup mushrooms, quartered
6 garlic cloves, minced

1 tbsp rosemary, fresh if possible
1 tbsp oregano
1 tbsp basil, fresh if possible
1 tsp salt
1 tsp pepper

8 sheets phyllo pastry
1/2 cup butter
1 cup goat cheese (or feta), crumbled
1/2 cup kalamata olives, pitted
1/2 cup sun-dried tomatoes, chopped
1 1/2 cups balsamic vinegar
2 tbsp honey

METHOD

In a roasting pan, toss red peppers, eggplant, red onion, zucchini, mushrooms and garlic in olive oil and bake in a 350°F oven for 20 minutes or until roasted. Let cool and add salt, pepper, oregano, rosemary, basil, crumbled goat cheese, olives and sun-dried tomatoes. Toss together gently. Make a stack of 4 sheets of phyllo brushing each sheet lightly with the butter. Arrange half of vegetable mixture down the middle of the phyllo lengthways and roll up in a cylinder, tucking in the ends. Repeat with remaining 4 sheets of phyllo and the rest of the filling. Place both strudels on a large cookie sheet and bake in a 400°F oven for 20-25 minutes. To prepare balsamic reduction, put balsamic vinegar and honey in a small saucepan over medium heat and let reduce until "syrupy", about 15 minutes. To assemble strudel, slice into portions and drizzle with sauce.

Our "Magic Mondays" are a really popular program offered at Whitewater throughout the season, which includes a lift ticket, lesson, ski rentals and a fabulous lunch. Check it out at the Whitewater Snow School.

SALSAS, CHUTNEYS, and SAUCES

because it's all about the sauce!

SUN-DRIED TOMATO AND FENNEL CHUTNEY

This chutney is especially good with our crab cakes and can also be served with samosas, chicken, lamb, or grilled fish.

makes 1 1/2 cups

INGREDIENTS

1 inch piece of ginger peeled, chopped, or grated

2 garlic cloves, finely diced

1 large shallot or 1/2 cup white onion, diced

1 cup fennel bulb, diced

3 tbsp lemon juice

1/2 cup white wine vinegar

3/4 cup sugar

1 cup fresh roma tomatoes, diced

2 tbsp sun-dried tomatoes, quartered

1 stick cinnamon

1 piece allspice or 1/2 tsp ground allspice

1 whole clove or 1/2 tsp ground cloves

1/2 cup dried apricots, finely chopped

METHOD

Place ginger, garlic, shallots, fennel and lemon juice in a food processor and grind to a paste. Set aside. In a heavy bottomed pot, combine vinegar and sugar. Bring to a simmer. Add roma tomatoes, sun-dried tomatoes, cinnamon, dried apricots, allspice, and cloves. Bring to a simmer again while stirring. Add the ginger paste to the pot and mix well. Simmer for 30-40 minutes until thick, stirring often to prevent sticking. Pour the chutney into a covered container and refrigerate. The flavour is more intense if made a day before serving.

RAITA

This is a classic and refreshing side dish to a spicy Indian feast!

makes 3 cups

INGREDIENTS

2 cups plain yogurt (regular not low-fat yogurt is best)
2 tsp ground cumin
1 large English cucumber, diced
3 tsp fresh or dried mint
1 cup tomato, diced and seeded
salt and pepper to taste

METHOD

Seed and coarsely dice cucumber and drain in colander to remove moisture. In a large mixing bowl, combine yogurt, cumin, mint, salt, pepper and tomato. Mix in the drained cucumber.

We use Raita on our Indian Chicken Burger and on top of our Sri Lankan Chicken Curry, both recipes can be found in the "Savouries" section.

ROASTED CORN AND RED PEPPER SALSA

We've served this on the Santa Fe Chicken Burger for years and now you'll find it in our very popular "Runaway Train Wrap".

makes 4 cups

INGREDIENTS

2 cups frozen corn
1 cup roasted red pepper, diced
1/2 cup red onion, diced
1/3 cup cilantro, chopped
juice and zest of 2 limes
2 tbsp olive oil
1 tsp cumin
1 tsp chili powder
1 tbsp brown sugar

METHOD

In a baking dish, toss corn in olive oil and brown sugar, and roast in a 350°F oven until "caramelized", about 20 minutes. Remove from oven and add the remaining ingredients. Mix well and keep covered in the refrigerator.

Excellent with grilled fish, chicken, or beef.

Cooked black beans and chopped fresh tomatoes make a great addition – add one additional cup for this recipe. With these additions, it can be served as a salad!

MANGOCHUTNEY

Serve with our Samosas and as a garnish for The Ymir Bowl.

makes about 2 cups

INGREDIENTS

1/4 cup brown sugar

1/4 cup white vinegar

1/3 cup raisins

4 whole cloves

1/2 tsp nutmeg

1/2 tsp cinnamon

pinch of salt

1 small onion, finely chopped

2 cups mango, coarsely chopped, fresh or frozen

2 tbsp water

2 tbsp fresh lime juice

METHOD

In saucepan, combine sugar, vinegar, raisins, cloves, nutmeg, cinnamon, salt and onion. Bring to a boil, then reduce to a low simmer for about 10 minutes. Add mango and water and simmer until thick, stirring often. Remove from heat and stir in lime juice. Will keep for up to one week when refrigerated.

Substitute chopped apples, pears, plums, or pineapple for the mangos.

ROASTED RED PEPPER HUMMUS

The secret ingredient in our "Million Dollar Sandwich." The tallest and healthiest sandwich on the menu – this one is really worth a million dollars!

makes about 2 cups

INGREDIENTS

1-14 oz can chickpeas, drained
1/4 cup olive oil
1/4 cup tahini paste (sesame seed paste)
3 garlic cloves, minced
1/4 cup fresh lemon juice
1/2 cup roasted red peppers
salt and pepper to taste

METHOD

In a food processor, place all ingredients and purée until smooth. Will keep refrigerated for up to six days.

Our Million Dollar Sandwich consists of Johnny's Multi-grain bread, red pepper hummus, provolone cheese, grated carrots, beets, sprouts, cucumbers, tomatoes, red onions and "Antoinette's Dip", which can be found at the Kootenay Co-op.

TZATZIKISAUCE

A Greek classic, served on our Souvlaki, Falafel, and Lamb Burgers.

makes 4 cups

INGREDIENTS

1 long English cucumber grated and juice drained through a colander
1 cup sour cream
2 cups plain yogurt
zest and juice of 1 lemon
2 garlic cloves, minced
1 tbsp dill, finely chopped (fresh if possible)
1/2 tsp mint (optional)
1 tsp salt
1/2 tsp pepper

METHOD

In a large mixing bowl, combine ingredients and mix well.

To thicken up thin yogurt, line a colander with paper towel and place it over a bowl.
Put the yogurt in the colander and let the liquid drip out for about an hour.

PAPAYAMANGOSALSA

This salsa is served on our Sante Fe Chicken Burger.
A perfect summer time accompaniment for grilled salmon or tuna!

makes 3 cups

INGREDIENTS

1 mango, diced
1 papaya, diced
2 red peppers, diced
1/2 red onion, diced
1 jalapeno pepper, seeded and finely diced
1 cup cilantro, chopped
1 tsp cumin
1 tsp chili powder
zest and juice of 1 lime
1/2 tsp salt

METHOD

In a large mixing bowl, mix all ingredients together. Store in refrigerator for up
to 2 days.

*This beautiful Salsa will look even prettier if you try to dice the mango, papaya, red
pepper and red onion in small even pieces.*

JALAPENOPEPPERJELLY

A recipe originated by Panny, passed on to my friend Maureen and then to us! Thanks gals!

makes approximately 6-6oz jars

INGREDIENTS

3 bell peppers (red is best) stems removed and seeded
1-7oz jar jalapeno peppers, drained and seeded if possible
6 1/2 cups white sugar
1 1/2 cups white or apple cider vinegar
2 packs liquid Certo

METHOD

Place bell peppers and jalapeno peppers in food processor and process until smooth. Transfer the peppers to a large heavy bottomed pot and add sugar and vinegar. Cook over medium heat until it reaches a boil. Simmer and stir for 8-10 minutes. Add two packs of liquid Certo and cook for 5 more minutes. Skim froth if desired. Pour into clean jars and put on lids. Jelly will set in about 3 hours and will keep for about 4 months.

A staple sandwich condiment at our house...so good with just about anything! Try it with grilled fish or chicken, or on a cracker with some really good cheese.

ORIENTAL EGGPLANT SPREAD

A delicious dip served with Black Sesame Rice crackers or some crusty bread and a glass of wine.

makes approximately 2 cups

INGREDIENTS

1 large eggplant
4 cloves garlic, minced
1 tbsp ginger, minced
2 tbsp vegetable oil
2 tbsp soy sauce
2 tbsp brown sugar

1 tsp chili paste
1 tsp rice vinegar
1 tbsp water
4 green onions, diced
1 tsp sesame oil
2 tbsp chopped cilantro

METHOD

Prick eggplant with a fork and place on baking pan and roast in a 350°F oven until soft, about 40 minutes. When it's cool enough to handle, cut it in half, scoop out the flesh and chop roughly. In a skillet, sauté garlic and ginger in oil till softened and fragrant. Add soy sauce, chili paste, brown sugar, rice vinegar and water.
Add eggplant, green onions, cilantro and sesame oil and cook for just a few minutes until everything is combined.

This is also great on Lamb Burgers.

CRANBERRY SALSA

There's no reason why cranberry sauce needs to be shaped like a can. This is the perfect salsa for Christmas or Thanksgiving, and don't forget tomorrow's turkey sandwich!

makes 2 cups

INGREDIENTS

1 1/2 cups fresh cranberries
1/3 cup white sugar
2 green onions, chopped
1/4 cup fresh cilantro
juice and zest of 1 lime
1 jalapeno pepper, seeded
2 tsp fresh grated ginger
pinch of salt

METHOD

In food processor, process cranberries until coarsely chopped but not pureed. Add remaining ingredients and process another 5-10 seconds. Keep covered in the refrigerator.

If fresh cranberries aren't available, frozen whole cranberries work just fine.

ROASTED GARLIC AIOLI

Good on burgers, sandwiches and as a dip for French Fries!

makes 2 cups

INGREDIENTS

2 cups good quality mayonnaise
1 whole garlic head
1/2 tsp olive oil
1/2 tsp rosemary or thyme
salt and pepper

METHOD

Cut the top of the garlic off to expose the flesh a little. Lay on a piece of tin foil and drizzle with olive oil and rosemary or thyme. Season with salt and pepper. Wrap foil around garlic to form a package. Roast in a 325ºF oven for 30-40 minutes. Squeeze garlic flesh out of skins and mash in a bowl with a fork until a smooth paste. Whisk in mayonnaise until blended. Taste for salt and pepper and season accordingly.

PUTTANESCA SAUCE

The story goes that the "Puttane" (Italian ladies of the night) developed this recipe because they were short on time but still wanted a good meal when they got home. We feel the same way, and it's one of our favourite pasta sauces!

serves 4

INGREDIENTS

1/2 cup extra virgin olive oil
1 can (2 ounces) anchovy fillets, drained
1/2 tsp dried chili flakes
4 cloves of garlic, crushed
2 cans (35 ounces) good quality plum tomato fillets, undrained
1 jar (2.5 ounces) capers, drained
1/2 cup pitted kalamata olives, coarsely chopped
fresh ground black pepper
2 tbsp flat leaf parsley, roughly chopped
freshly grated parmesan cheese for garnish

METHOD

In a medium sized saucepan over low heat, gently sauté and mash the anchovies, garlic, chili flakes and oil to form a paste. Add the tomato fillets, capers and olives. Stir while sauce comes to a bubbling simmer. Reduce heat to low. Simmer uncovered, for about an hour stirring occasionally. Season with pepper. Just before serving add parsley. Garnish with parmesan cheese. This recipe can easily be doubled. It freezes well. Serve with linguine or spaghetti.

This sauce is really good the next day on some bread or good crackers.

OUR FAMOUS BURGER SAUCE

...no laughing now!

makes 1 1/2 cups

INGREDIENTS

1 cup good quality mayonnaise
1/4 cup Bull's Eye or Runaway Train BBQ Sauce
1/4 cup dill pickles, chopped finely
1/2 tsp chile in adobo sauce

METHOD

In a mixing bowl, mix together all ingredients. This sauce will keep for up to 2 weeks when refrigerated.

It's excellent on any burger and my kid's like it in their sandwiches too...

PEPPERCORN, BRANDY AND GORGONZOLA SAUCE

A roast beef dinner at my house wouldn't be complete
without this addition.

makes 2 cups

INGREDIENTS

1 onion, diced
1/4 cup butter
1/2 cup green peppercorns,
drained and rinsed
1 1/2 cups brandy
2 cups beef stock or demi-glace

1 cup whipping cream
1 tbsp maple syrup
2 tbsp Dijon mustard
2 tbsp crumbled gorgonzola cheese

METHOD

Saute onion in butter until soft. Add peppercorns and brandy and cook on medium
heat until brandy has reduced by half. Add stock and reduce again for half an hour on
medium heat. Keep simmering and add whipping cream, maple syrup and Dijon
mustard. Let reduce again until sauce is thick enough to coat the back of a spoon. Stir
in the gorgonzola cheese.

Serve on steaks, roast beef, lamb chops, grilled chicken breasts or pork tenderloin.
Because...It's all about the sauce!!!

SWEET THINGS

our favourites

WHITEWATERMARVELLOUSMUFFINS

So here it is...the Basic WH2O Muffin recipe! Doctor it up any way you want to.

makes 24 muffins

INGREDIENTS

1 cup soft margarine or butter

3 cups sugar

1 tbsp vanilla

6 eggs (room temperature)

1 1/2 cups buttermilk

7 1/2 cups flour

2 tbsp baking powder

1 1/2 tsp baking soda

1 1/2 tsp salt

2 cups sliced pears

1 cup chopped white chocolate

1/2 cup finely chopped crystallized ginger

METHOD

In a mixing bowl, cream together margarine, sugar and vanilla. Beat in eggs and buttermilk. In a separate bowl, mix together flour, baking powder, baking soda and salt. Combine wet and dry ingredients. Quickly mix in the pears, white chocolate and ginger, reserving a little of each to place on top of the muffins before they go in the oven. Grease muffin tins and fill 2/3 with mixture. Top with reserved ingredients. Bake in a 350°F oven until they are done. (approximately 30 minutes).

Try different combinations...If using frozen fruit, don't thaw first. Dried cherry and dark chocolate, raspberry and hazelnut, cranberry and toasted almond, blueberry and lemon zest...

WHITEWATER CINNAMON BUNS

Sweet & gooey and as essential as fresh powder to some of our dedicated regulars.

makes 12 buns

INGREDIENTS

1/3 cup butter at room temperature

2/3 cup brown sugar

2 tsp salt

2 eggs

2/3 cup milk

1 1/8 cups warm water

2 tbsp active dry yeast

5-6 cups flour

4 tbsp butter, melted

3/4 cup brown sugar

2 tbsp cinnamon

1/2 cup pecans

1/2 cup raisins

METHOD

In a small bowl dissolve the yeast in the warm water. Let sit for 5 minutes until the yeast is bubbly. In a large mixing bowl, cream together butter, 2/3 cup brown sugar and salt. Add eggs one at a time. Mix in milk, dissolved yeast mixture and flour, 1 cup at a time mixing until smooth. Add enough flour to make soft dough. Turn onto a lightly floured board. Knead dough until smooth and springy, about 10 minutes, adding more flour if needed. Place in a large greased bowl, cover and let rise in a warm place until doubled in size, approximately 45 minutes. Punch down. Roll out into a large rectangular shape, about 12 x 18 inches. Brush with melted butter and remaining brown sugar. Sprinkle with cinnamon, pecans and raisins. Roll lengthwise into a big log and slice into 1 1/2 inch pieces. Place slices in a greased 9 x 13 inch pan about one inch apart. Let rise for another 45 minutes. Bake in a 350°F oven for approximately 45 minutes. Let cool and ice with your favourite butter icing.

FRESH TRACKS CORN BREAD

...Great with our Vegetarian Black Bean Chili and Jalapeno Jelly Butter!

Serves 10-12

INGREDIENTS

2 cups onions, diced

1/2 cup red pepper, diced

1/2 cup green pepper, diced

1 small jalapeno pepper, minced

1 cup chopped cilantro

2 cups frozen corn

1 cup vegetable oil

5 eggs

1 cup cheddar cheese, grated

1/2 cup brown sugar

1 cup cornmeal

1 cup flour

1 tsp salt

1 1/2 tbsp baking powder

1 tsp ground black pepper

METHOD

In a skillet, sauté onions and peppers until softened. Place in large mixing bowl and let cool a bit. Beat the eggs with the oil until well combined. Whisk together the flour, cornmeal, brown sugar, baking powder, salt and pepper. Add the egg and oil mixture along with the corn and cilantro to the cooled vegetables. Quickly fold in the dry ingredients and the cheese. Put the batter in a greased 10 inch round cake pan or a 9x13 inch rectangular pan. Bake in a 350°F oven for approximately 30 minutes, or until golden and firm on top.

To prepare Jalapeno Jelly Butter - just combine 1/2 cup jalapeno jelly with 1/2 cup soft butter.

WHITEWATERBROWNIES

Fudgy, chewy, and crunchy all in the same bite! After much recipe tasting, this is definitely our favourite brownie. Mel Gibson loved them when he was working in Vancouver on "Bird on a Wire".

makes 9 large brownies

INGREDIENTS

8 ounces semi-sweet chocolate

1/4 cup butter

2 large eggs

1/2 cup brown sugar

2 tsp vanilla

5 tbsp sour cream

3/4 cup flour

1 tsp baking powder

1/2 cup semi-sweet chocolate chips

METHOD

Melt semi-sweet chocolate and butter together in a double boiler over warm water. Let cool slightly. In a large bowl, whisk together eggs, brown sugar and vanilla until just blended. Add melted butter and chocolate and blend again. Blend in sour cream, then add flour and baking powder until just incorporated. Finish with chocolate chips. Pour into greased 8" x 8" pan and bake in a 350°F oven for 20-25 minutes.

A drizzle of White Chocolate and a Chocolate dipped Strawberry on top turns these into an elegant dessert!

PECANSQUARES

Couldn't resist including this recipe because they taste so good!

makes about 12

INGREDIENTS

CRUST
1 cup cold butter
6 tbsp brown sugar
3 cups flour
1 egg
1 tsp lemon juice
3 cups pecans, whole

FILLING
1 cup butter
2/3 cup honey
1 cup brown sugar
4 tbsp whipping cream

METHOD

Place butter, sugar, flour, egg and lemon juice in food processor and process until mixture just holds together, but is still crumbly. Press into prepared 9" x 13" pan and bake in a 350°F for 15 minutes or until golden brown. Arrange whole pecans on top of prepared crust. To prepare filling, melt together butter, honey and sugar in a saucepan. Let boil for 5-7 minutes, stirring constantly. Remove from heat and add cream. Drizzle filling over pecans until completely covered. Return to oven and bake for 20 minutes. When cool, cut into squares.

Chocolate chips can be added on top as soon as they come out of the oven, if desired.

WHITEWATERGRANOLABARS

Easy, delicious, and the ideal backpack snack!

Makes 16 big bars

INGREDIENTS

1 cup butter

1 1/2 cups peanut butter

1 1/2 tbsp vanilla

2 cups brown sugar

1 cup corn syrup

6 cups oats

1 cup coconut, toasted

1 cup sunflower seeds, toasted

1 cup sesame seeds, toasted

2 cups chocolate chips (or 1 cup raisins and 1 cup chocolate chips)

METHOD

In a skillet, toast coconut, sunflower seeds and sesame seeds and set aside to cool. In a large mixing bowl, cream together butter, peanut butter, vanilla and brown sugar. Add corn syrup and then mix in remaining ingredients. Press into greased 12 x 18 inch cookie sheet. Bake in a 350°F oven for approximately 20 minutes or until golden brown. Let cool slightly and cut while still warm.

Substitute toasted almonds and 1 tsp almond extract for the sunflower seeds and vanilla if you want to switch it up a little.

JOEY'S APPLE CAKE

Another tried and true recipe from Jo.
A gorgeous fall cake, which seems to taste even better the next day.

Serves 10 - 12

INGREDIENTS

CAKE

3 cups flour
1 1/2 cups white sugar
1/2 cup brown sugar
3 tsp cinnamon
1 tsp baking soda
3/4 tsp nutmeg
1/2 tsp salt
3/4 cup butter, melted
3/4 cup vegetable oil

3 eggs
3 tsp vanilla or almond extract
4 cups apples, peeled and diced
1/2 cup pecans (optional)

CARAMEL SAUCE

1/4 cup butter
1 cup packed brown sugar
3/4 cup whipping cream

METHOD

In a large mixing bowl, combine flour, sugars, cinnamon, baking soda, nutmeg and salt. In a separate bowl, combine melted butter, oil, eggs and extract. Stir wet ingredients into dry ingredients until just combined. Fold in apples and pecans. Spoon batter into a greased and floured Bundt pan and bake in a 325°F oven for 1 hour, or until a toothpick inserted in the centre comes out clean. Cool in pan for approximately 15 minutes, unmold and cool on rack. To make caramel sauce, melt butter and sugar over medium heat stirring for about 5 minutes until the sugar is dissolved. Add the cream, stirring as you bring to a boil. Simmer until the mixture is slightly reduced and thickened, about 10 minutes. Slice cake and serve with warm caramel sauce and a scoop of vanilla ice cream.

KIM'S MOM'S **CHOCOLATE** OATMEAL **CAKE**

There are a million chocolate cake recipes out there – This is the one we make for all our staff parties. We've used it for wedding cakes, for Black Forest Cake, kid's birthday cakes...
A friend from my movie catering days shared this recipe and it has been passed on to many for over 20 years!

serves 8

INGREDIENTS

1/2 cup oats
1 cup boiling water
1/2 cup butter, room temperature
1 1/2 cups brown sugar
2 eggs

1 tsp vanilla
1 cup flour
1 tsp baking soda
1 tsp baking powder
1/3 cup cocoa powder
1/2 tsp salt

METHOD

Pour boiling water into a small mixing bowl with oats. Let stand 10 minutes. In a large mixing bowl, mix butter and sugar together until light and creamy. Add eggs one at a time, then vanilla. In another bowl, sift together flour, baking soda, baking powder, cocoa powder and salt. Alternating wet and dry, add oat mixture and dry ingredients to creamed butter mixture in three parts. Stir after each addition until smooth. Pour batter into a greased 9 inch springform pan. Bake at 350°F for approximately 30 minutes until skewer inserted into middle of cake comes out clean. Ice with your favourite icing or cover in whipped cream!

This recipe doubles beautifully to fit into a 12 1/2 inch round cake pan and feeds at least 16 and more, if some of them are little ones.

CREAMSCONES

These scones are beautiful, light and delicious. You can add fruit and other goodies to them but we think some things are perfect just the way they are!

serves 12

INGREDIENTS

3 cups flour

2 tbsp baking powder

1 tbsp sugar

1 tsp salt

6 tbsp cold butter, cut into cubes

3 eggs

3/4 cup whipping cream

METHOD

Preheat oven to 400°F. In a medium bowl, sift together flour, baking powder, salt and sugar. Using a pastry cutter or two knives cut in the cold butter until the pieces are the size of small peas. In a small bowl lightly beat the eggs. Stir in the cream. Add this mixture all at once to the dry ingredients gently incorporating until the mixture forms a sticky dough. If the dough seems a bit dry add more cream. Don't overwork. Turn the dough onto a lightly floured board. Gently pat the dough into a rough circle about 1 inch thick. Using a 3 inch biscuit cutter make 12 scones. Place on baking sheet 2 inches apart. Brush tops of scones with cream and sprinkle lightly with sugar. Bake for about 12 to 15 minutes until scones are a beautiful golden brown.

Variations: try berries, dried fruit, nuts, orange zest, lemon zest or chocolate chips. No more than 1 cup total. Just add after you mix in the wet ingredients and be gentle - don't overmix.

Serve hot out of the oven with lots of butter and your favourite homemade jam.

GAIL'S FAMOUS
CHOCOLATE CHIP COOKIES

Our dear friend Gail, from our movie catering days, used to make these cookies a lot. She'd have to hide them while they were cooling because everyone on set would smell them and leave the scene to head for her cookies!

makes 24 cookies

INGREDIENTS

1 cup shortening (Crisco is best)
3/4 cup brown sugar
1/4 cup white sugar
1 tsp vanilla
1 tsp baking soda
1/3 cup boiling water

1 1/2 cups flour
1/2 tsp salt
2 cups large flake oats
1 cup chocolate chips
1/2 cup walnuts or sunflower seeds

METHOD

In a large mixing bowl, cream together the shortening, sugars and vanilla until light. Dissolve baking soda in boiling water. Add to the batter and mix well. Incorporate flour, salt and mix until combined. Fold in oats, chocolate chips and nuts or seeds. Place spoonfuls of batter onto greased cookie sheets and press with fork until cookie shaped. Bake in a 350°F oven for 10–12 minutes.

PECAN FRUIT MUFFINS

These are the muffins we like to make at home – everybody likes the nice streusel topping.

makes 18 muffins

INGREDIENTS

STREUSEL TOPPING
1/4 cup pecans, chopped
(toasted is always better)
1/4 cup flour
1/4 cup white sugar
1/4 cup butter

MUFFINS
3 eggs
1 1/2 tsp vanilla
1 cup vegetable oil
2 cups brown sugar
2 1/2 cups diced fruit or berries
(if using frozen, don't thaw first)
1/2 cup pecans, chopped
2 cups flour
1/2 cup corn meal

1/2 cup oats
2 tsp baking soda
1/2 tsp baking powder
1/2 tsp cinnamon
1/2 tsp salt
1/2 tsp allspice
1/2 tsp nutmeg

METHOD

In food processor chop pecans, flour, sugar and butter until fine. Set aside. To prepare muffins, beat together eggs, oil, sugar and vanilla in a large mixing bowl, until thick and foamy. Stir in fruit and nuts. In another bowl, stir together all dry ingredients. Gradually add to fruit mixture, stirring gently just to blend. Spoon into greased muffin tins. Sprinkle some of the streusel topping over each muffin and bake in a 350°F oven for 25-30 minutes.

TEX'S CARROT CAKE

Thanks to Tex and Edith Mowatt for all the years of friendship
and support. This cake is their favourite!

serves 16-18

INGREDIENTS

CAKE

3 cups flour

2 tsp baking powder

2 tsp baking soda

4 tsp cinnamon

1 tsp salt

1 1/2 cups brown sugar

1 cup raisins

1 cup walnuts, chopped

1 1/4 cups oil

4 eggs, slightly beaten

2 cups carrots, grated

1 cup crushed pineapple, drained

2 tsp vanilla

CREAM CHEESE ICING

1 cup cream cheese, softened

1/2 cup butter, softened

2 tsp vanilla

6 cups icing sugar

METHOD

In a large bowl, combine flour, baking powder, baking soda, cinnamon, and salt. Stir in sugar, raisins, and walnuts. Make a well and add oil, carrots, pineapple, vanilla, and eggs. Blend well. Pour into a greased 9 or 10 inch round baking pan and bake in a 350°F oven for approximately 1 hour until skewer inserted into center comes out clean. Cool. To prepare icing, beat together room temperature cream cheese and butter until light and fluffy. Add vanilla and icing sugar and continue beating until smooth. Cut the cake in half horizontally and spread some icing between the two layers, before icing the whole cake.

Orange or lemon zest or a bit of Grand Marnier make a happy addition to the icing! Recipe easily doubles so use it for a wedding cake or a big party.

GINGER LIME CHEESECAKE

An old favourite cheesecake recipe from my sweet sister Clare...

Serves 8-10

INGREDIENTS

CRUST
1 1/2 cups graham wafer crumbs
1/3 cup butter, melted
3 tbsp sugar

FILLING
2-250g packs cream cheese
1/2 cup sugar
2 eggs
2 tsp fresh lime juice
1 tsp ginger, freshly grated

TOPPING
1 1/2 cups sour cream
5 tbsp sugar
2 tbsp crystallized ginger, cut into slivers

METHOD

Combine graham wafer crumbs, sugar and melted butter in a bowl. Press the crumbs into a 9 inch springform or fluted tart pan. Prebake crust in 350°F oven for 8-10 minutes. Combine cream cheese, sugar, lime juice and ginger in food processor. Process until well mixed. Add eggs and process 10 seconds more. Pour filling into cooled crust and bake for 20-25 minutes. To prepare topping, mix sour cream, sugar and the crystallized ginger together. Spread over filling. Turn off oven and return the cake to the oven for 10 minutes. Remove and chill before serving.

For the total ginger experience, you can substitute ginger snap cookie crumbs for the graham wafers.

CRACKLE TOP SNOWY
MOUNTAIN COOKIES

A tender and intensely flavoured chocolate cookie coated with sweet white powdery snow. For many, this is true cookie perfection.

makes 4 dozen cookies

INGREDIENTS

8 ounces good semi sweet dark chocolate (Callebaut)
1 1/4 cups flour
1/2 cup cocoa powder
2 tsp baking powder
1/4 tsp salt

1/2 cup butter
1 1/3 cups packed light brown sugar
2 large eggs
1 tsp vanilla
1/3 cup milk
1 cup icing sugar

METHOD

Coarsely chop chocolate and melt over a pan of simmering water. Set aside to cool. Sift together flour, cocoa, baking powder and salt. Beat butter and light brown sugar until light and fluffy, 3 to 4 minutes. Add eggs and vanilla and beat until well combined. Add the cooled melted chocolate. Add flour alternately with milk. When the dough comes together shape into a flattened disk and wrap with plastic wrap. Chill for at least 2 hours, until the dough is firm. Using 1 heaping teaspoon of dough, shape into 1 inch balls. Roll each ball in icing sugar until completely coated. If any cocoa coloured dough is visible, roll in sugar again. Place cookies on a parchment paper covered cookie sheet 2 inches apart. Make sure they don't roll around when you put them in the oven. Bake in a 350°F oven until flat and the sugar coating (snow) splits, 12-15 minutes. Let them cool completely then store in an airtight tin for up to 2 weeks. Or eat them all right away with your family and friends.

This is my little friend Noah's favourite cookie and he likes to pop them in his mouth whole, so that none of the (snow) falls on him!

WHITE CHOCOLATE HAZELNUT BROWNIES

This one comes from my friend Marianne, a great camping and catering partner. We sell a lot of these – especially if they're drizzled with dark chocolate!

makes 10-12 brownies

INGREDIENTS

1 cup butter

10 oz good quality white chocolate, chopped into small pieces

1 1/4 cups sugar

4 large eggs room temperature

1 tbsp vanilla

2 cups flour

1/2 tsp salt

1 cup hazelnuts, coarsely chopped and toasted*

METHOD

Place butter and chocolate in a large metal bowl in the oven at a low temperature of 225°F. Stir occasionally until incorporated. Remove from oven. Turn oven up to 325°F. Stir sugar into melted chocolate. Add eggs and vanilla and mix well. It may look "curdled". Add flour, salt and toasted hazelnuts and quickly stir until just mixed. Pour batter into a 9" x 13" prepared pan. Bake in a 325°F oven for 30-35 minutes or until top is light brown, but centre is soft. Cool completely before cutting. Sprinkle with icing sugar, or drizzle with dark chocolate.

*To toast hazelnuts: place nuts on a cookie sheet in a 350°F oven and toast until skins look like they're falling off – approximately 15 minutes. Remove from oven and pour nuts into a clean tea towel and roll until much of the skin has fallen off.

HEALTHY FRIDGE MUFFINS

Another great recipe from Cathy Crooks. When you wake up in the morning just plop the batter in the muffin tins and bake. You'll have the perfect snack to eat in your car on your way up to the mountain.

makes 12 muffins

INGREDIENTS

1 cup whole wheat flour
1 cup all purpose flour
3 cups oats
4 tsp baking powder
1 tsp baking soda
2 tsp cinnamon
2 whole eggs

2 egg whites
2 cups yogurt
2 tbsp canola oil
1/3 cup honey
1/2 cup grated apples
1/4 cup grated carrots
1/4 cup raisins

THE DRIZZLE
2 tbsp honey
2 tbsp apple juice or fresh orange juice

METHOD

Combine wet ingredients in a very large mixing bowl. Combine dry ingredients together well and add to the wet mixture. Leave in the refrigerator overnight in a covered bowl. In the morning add the grated apples, carrots and raisins to the batter. Fill muffins tins and bake in a 350°F oven for 30 minutes. Heat the honey and juice and drizzle over the tops of the muffins while they are still warm.

THANKS MIKE

For always being there...